2

For SDG

....Such a help when I was going through it!
With Love

Supporting the Move to Secondary School

A Handbook for Parent and Pupil

by

Kate Stewart and Elizabeth Ishka

Emerald Guides
www. emeraldpublishing.co.uk

Emerald Guides
Brighton BN2 4EG

ISBN 978 1847161 44 4

Printed by GN Printing Essex

Cover design by Straightforward Graphics

Whilst every effort has been made to ensure that the information
contained within this book is correct at the time of going to
press, the author and publisher can take no responsibility for the
errors or omissions contained within.

Supporting the Move to Secondary School

A Handbook for Parent and Pupil

by

Kate Stewart and Elizabeth Ishka

The book is a guide for parent and child on ways to support and manage the move from Primary to Secondary School. This can be an anxious time for many children and parents may feel unsure about the best ways to help.

This book provides practical advice on how to manage the transition: from preparing beforehand to providing strategies through the holiday and supporting and coping through the early days at the new school.

It gives parents a whole range of ways to help and gives both parent and child confidence to navigate through this potentially challenging time.

CONTENTS

CONTENTS

Supporting the Move to Secondary School

A Handbook for Parent and Pupil

Part One: So what's the problem?

How is Secondary School going to be different?

How Secondary School is going to be different:

Size

Most Secondary Schools are considerably larger than most Primary Schools. Where Primary Schools may be local, they may then all feed, from a considerable area, into one Secondary School. This means that where your child may now be one of fewer than 300 pupils in the school, he/she may soon be one of closer to 3,000. The sheer scale of this is daunting.

In actual fact, apart from the sheer geographical size of the new school, its size in pupil numbers may have a far smaller impact than your child might imagine. He/she is still likely to be in classes of, say, 30 pupils, and the fact that there are one hundred similar sized classes at any one time, rather than of only ten, doesn't really make much difference to him/her. Indeed the size and scale of the buildings may be more manageable than he/she imagines, too, as he/she will soon learn his/her 'bits' of it, and not know, nor need to know, other parts.

What will impact on him (in the interests of concision will henceforth in general refer to the child in the third person masculine – no sexism intended!) is the fact that with so large a school, most people will not know him. This means that, for example, he may have to spell an unusual surname or correct pronunciation of a forename countless times. In essence, it means that there is less room for him as an *individual* and he will be treated more like a cog in the infrastructure as a whole. For most children this doesn't matter too much. They learn that a certain behaviour is what Year 7s are expected to do and then do it or choose not to do it according to character. For some though it is more complicated. If your child has some sort of difference, if he has some special needs for example, or wishes to keep certain religious observances, he is going to have to work harder than before to get his needs or wishes across.

Whereas at his old school staff were aware he became claustrophobic in crowds and allowed him to stand to the side of large groups, he may have to explain again and again in his new school. If he wishes to keep a fast as part of his religious observance he is going to have to contend with lunchtime staff, home economic teachers and the like for himself. In other words, he is going to have to learn to articulate his individuality if he is to get it recognised and this may be fairly daunting.

How Secondary School is going to be different:

Teachers

Another difference is in the teachers. Contrary to popular rumour the Secondary School teacher is not an ogre but nor is he quite the same beast as the Primary School teacher. In essence, the Primary School teacher has chosen to *teach* children; the Secondary School teacher has chosen to *teach his subject* to children. The difference is a subtle one but nevertheless essential. Secondary School teachers are specialists, with a particular interest and expertise in a particular subject. They have chosen to teach children (although in this case 'children' extends right up to eighteen year olds) but their interest may be less in the development of the child as a whole person and more in that child's development in, for example, mathematics. Nor do they spend all day with the same children. Where the Primary School teacher knows that young Carl's parents are going through a rough patch and keeps an eye out for (and makes allowance for) disturbed behaviour in Carl, the Secondary music teacher may only meet Carl for half an hour a fortnight and is probably not going to make allowances for Carl's outbursts in quite the same way.

Of course, tutors do try their best to share pertinent information about individual children with all of their teachers but the system is simply not set up to the same extent for all teachers to know the needs of all children in quite the same way as would happen organically in the smaller scale Primary School milieu.

Another issue about all these different teachers is that they will all have slightly different rules and expectations. The child has to learn to remember that Mr W likes you to line up outside his classroom, where Mrs X wants you to go in, take a seat and start working. Miss Y allows you to sit where you like but Dr Z insists that you sit in alphabetical order according to the register. To complicate matters, Dr Z insists that homework be completed on A4 file paper and be ready to give in at the next lesson whereas Mr W likes you to work in your books and always allows a week. Mrs X gives detentions routinely if you are wearing trainers rather than school shoes but Miss Y takes her own shoes off and sits cross-legged on the desk. It is a lot to remember!

In the course of an ordinary week most pupils in Year 7 will have ten or more different teachers, each delivering different subjects and having different rules and expectations. Many of these will change term by term if the Year is following a 'carousel' arrangement, whereby they might have Food Technology for one term, Textiles for the next and Woodwork for the third. The following year all teachers will probably change as the year group moves on. What the child has to get used to is the business of being taught, rather than the familiarity of one teacher and one classroom. For most children this becomes a positive advantage as different teaching styles lead to different enthusiasms and successes but for some it can be a jolt to the system.

How Secondary School is going to be different:

Expectations of independence

It may also come as something of a shock at Secondary School that the child is more or less responsible for himself. Whereas at Primary School the message was "Ask your parents..." or "Take this letter home...", the message at Secondary School is very much one of making decisions for yourself. It is also about facing consequences for yourself.

If at Secondary School you are late, the excuse that your parent dropped you off late makes no difference. If at Secondary School you fail to bring in the ingredients required for a Food Tech lesson, saying your parents didn't go shopping will not prevent a sanction.

Although some frameworks remain in place, for example parent consent forms for some activities, getting paperwork signed is also the responsibility of the child. If your child does not get you to sign the form for the history trip in time, he may well find himself missing the activity; this is what growing up is all about.

How Secondary School is going to be different:

Work

The same is true to a great extent regarding work. Parents will be encouraged to take an interest in homework and to show some awareness of what work their child is doing. However, it is also accepted as time goes by that the child may be learning at a level higher than his parents have achieved so that relying on parental input is no longer appropriate. Most parents can listen to their child read when they first bring an early reading book home from Primary School in Year 1. Rather fewer will be able to help with quadratic equations or suggest procedure for a physics experiment or identify the need for a naturalised F sharp in the slow movement once their child is at Secondary School. Pupils therefore learn gradually to rely instead on their teachers, on each other and on themselves.

It is also true that children have to learn to accept the responsibility for failure as well. If the child is not keeping up, either through lack of ability in that subject or through lack of application, it is likely that he will be moved down a set, possibly not accepted for that subject when the time comes to choose his options (the courses he is to follow to exam stage) or possibly he may not be accepted into a certain exam group. If the problem is genuine lack of understanding some additional help may make all the difference. More worrying for parents though is that if their child's inability to get on is due to lack of application or attention there is little they can do other than try to understand the reasons behind their child's disengagement. To a far greater extent than in Primary education, a Secondary School child has to accept responsibility for his own successes and failures.

How Secondary School is going to be different:

Social

One of the biggest differences between Primary and Secondary School is in the relative importance to your child of the people involved. It may be fair to say that, for younger children, their parents and then their teacher are the people who have most influence over them. They are motivated largely by a wish to please these adults and acceptance by and approval from these people are strong factors in deciding what the child does or does not do.

At Secondary School this may well change. For one thing the child is no longer faced by just one teacher; several teachers, each seen for a relatively short time, may well exert a less significant influence over the child. The child may still prefer not to provoke disapproval and few children like to be told off but the motivation to please each individual teacher is unlikely to be as strong now that there are so many more to work with. Instead, as a natural part of growing up, your child is more likely to be influenced by a wish to be accepted by a peer group. Children decide which group they are going to belong to and acceptance by that group is a very strong influence indeed. Unfortunately if the presiding ethos of this group is to mess about in class then your child is likely to be more strongly affected by this peer pressure than by his motivation to please the teacher... or you. Who your child chooses as friends, how he perceives himself and with whom therefore he allies himself, can be a monumental factor in academic success or failure.

Part of this group (or gang) culture may include bullying. 'Gang' suggests to us a fearsome group intent on violence but in fact any group of pupils may be termed a gang. The ones who are into a certain sport, the ones who like particular computer games, the ones who play the classical guitar – each group may come together to form a group or gang. As such, each group may exclude others who are not in their group and may be rejected by other groups because of their membership of this one. Followers of one football team will tend to reject a follower of another team most vehemently, their 'differentness' becoming more powerful than the more obvious 'bonding' one of all being interested in the same sport.

A lot of taunting, name-calling, threatening, rejecting, ostracising and ridiculing behaviour at this age comes from this need to identify self with others and therefore to reject those who do not meet one's own criteria. This is the root of much bullying, particularly of the child whose group or gang is small or fragile (the classical guitar playing group, for example) or who has no group or gang at all.

The early years of Secondary School are not a comfortable time to be an outsider, to be different in some way and not to belong. Later, as the pupils reach young adulthood at Years 12 and 13, differentness is positively encouraged and individuality has a high premium. During these adolescent years however belonging is all and to be individual may just be seen as being 'odd' and, as such, without the protection of peers.

All children fear bullying. Perhaps what they fear as much as the physical threat is that being bullied means that they do not fit in and are not accepted. Bullying in whatever form it takes – physical, verbal or by being rejected and feeling left out – is frightening and soul-destroying and should ALWAYS be taken seriously.

The other huge change in the society children face at Secondary as opposed to Primary School is that it is populated by both boys and girls – a fact they may hardly yet have noticed when they were younger! Of course, some Secondary Schools are single sex but never believe that the other sex isn't mentioned, discussed and obsessed-over at these schools just as much (indeed, probably more so) than at mixed sex schools. At mixed sex school there is at least a possibility that your child will grow up aware that members of the opposite sex are just normal human beings who number half the planet's population. Some may, in time, even become friends. Some may, just possibly, become boy/girlfriends ...and this possibility is, perhaps understandably, enough to make concentrating on history lessons or the anatomy of a sheep's eye very challenging indeed!

How Secondary School is going to be different:

Dealing with a society

As the Secondary School pupil becomes more interested in his peers than in the adults around him so this may have an impact on the way he responds to those adults. Few Primary School pupils have much experience of a teacher being unable to keep order. On the whole in the Primary classroom the teacher is in charge and this brings security for everyone. Each pupil's contribution is given equal merit: no one is ridiculed for wrong answers and the adult controls the session and makes sure that everyone has an opportunity to take part and to learn. This may not always be the case in all lessons at Secondary School.

Although it is seldom discussed teacher control over some classes in Secondary Schools can be tenuous at best. Keeping the attention and interest of thirty or so disenchanted teenagers can be a very difficult task and most teachers on certain days, or at some point in their careers, have felt that control start to slip. For some of them this has become almost the norm. Usually these teachers will be given support from within the school and with further training, and with more experience, most will be able to be good teachers again. In the meantime though the class may no longer be under the control of an adult and – as everyone who has read Lord of The Flies will understand – rule by children is a frightening prospect. At best your child is unlikely to learn much in these lessons; at worst these lessons may actually become something to fear as the name calling and bullying that the teacher is supposed to stop become increasingly rife. It is also worth being aware as a parent that the geographical site of school may not be as safe at Secondary stage as it was at primary. At Primary School any adults who stray onto the site are likely to be recognised as strangers and their presence challenged. Most schools, both Primary and secondary, will these days have a security system to prevent strangers from accessing the building. Secondary School sites however may be very extensive and it may be difficult to patrol the furthest reaches. If outsiders are determined to access the playing fields for example – perhaps to sell cigarettes or alcohol or worse – this may be difficult for school staff to prevent. Staff are on duty during break times and some adults should be on duty during lunchtimes (although these may not be teaching staff) but challenging drug dealers, for example, may be quite understandably daunting for these adults. A school in this position is likely to be working very closely with police but it is nevertheless important as a parent to be alert to dangers of this kind and to make sure that you discuss such matters with your child and work together on strategies to stay safe.

A Secondary School forms a mini-society in its own right. Within this there may well be injustices. Your child may feel blamed for something he didn't do. He may be kept in for a detention because of the poor behaviour of others or may find that his genuine explanation for missing work is not listened to or accepted. Children (and adults!) find this very frustrating and may become very angry. It is important as parents that you listen to this anger and do not assume that your child is in the wrong. Taking your child seriously is part of accepting that he is growing up. Equally though the school needs your authority if it is to manage your child as part of this large and unwieldy mass. If your child is given a detention – and you genuinely believe this detention to be undeserved – it is still not helpful to anyone to merely refuse to give parental permission for your child to stay behind after school or even to encourage your child not to attend. If you believe there has been a genuine injustice make an appointment with your child's form teacher and discuss the matter calmly. Both your child and the school need to be confident that you will support the school in sanctions that are deserved. Once that confidence is fully established it should be easier to discuss the matter fruitfully if your child *has been* the victim of a false allegation...*or* punished without just cause...*or* there were mitigating circumstances of which the teacher was unaware.

How Secondary School is going to be different:

Being part of something that has nothing to do with

parents.

It is important the school and you form a united front not least because that forms a stable position from which your child can make his own decisions. Up until now his values have probably been your values. All sorts of opinions, from religion to politics, from which team to support to what clothes to wear, came initially from you. Your child is now part of a separate society away from your influence and he will have to make these decisions for himself. Your child may find this period of trying out of ideas quite difficult. If you are liberal minded, hearing your child saying things you find offensive – that are racist perhaps, or homophobic – will be distressing. Equally your child may start to have opinions which you find radical or revolutionary. On the whole these opinions are as likely to be stated as much for their shock-giving qualities as from genuine conviction and it probably best to react as little as possible. They may also be a reflection of the group your child has chosen to be a part of and you may have to keep an eye on this: some groups are more likely to be heading for trouble than others.

On the whole though, even if the content is alarming to you, this ability to explore beliefs independently is a good sign. As he grows up your child is going to have to sort out his own value system for himself – and begin to accept the consequences of his decisions. Will he choose to observe religious customs while at school? Would he speak up in defence of another person? Will he give in to the temptation to cheat in an exam? Your job as a parent is changing:- you are no longer there to give him all the answers but you are still there to guide. Perhaps most importantly you are there to pick up the pieces when he makes a wrong decision. Watching your offspring turn from a child into an adult is fascinating and rewarding as well as painful and poignant. The move from Primary to Secondary is the huge first step on this eminently exciting journey.

A word from Elizabeth, aged twelve:

"Hello. My name is Elizabeth and I have just started Year 8 so I remember what it was like to move to Secondary School last

year and have been helping our new Year 7s settle in this term. I have been asked to give some 'pupil perspective' on how to make 'moving up' go more smoothly and how to manage it all without getting in a total panic! I'll try to add something to each section giving you some feedback and advice from the pupil's point of view."

Supporting the Move to Secondary School

A Handbook for Parent and Pupil

Part Two: So what can we do to help?

Before Leaving Primary School:

Choosing your Secondary School and applying

Your first job, as parent of a soon-to-be-eleven-year-old, is to choose a Secondary School and your second is to get your child a place at it. These sound simple but the reality in many parts of the country is far from this! The business of getting your child into the 'best' school has become something of a national obsession and it would be naïve to say it isn't something many parents expend a great deal of effort to achieve. Of course we all wish the best for our children so this is scarcely surprising. Whatever way you look at it, it is something you are going to have to get your head around as your child grows older.

If your child is going to school locally your best source of information is probably going to be other parents. In this case you are all in the same boat and many a conversation in the

Primary School playground as we wait for our kids at the end of the day centres around what Secondary Schools are available locally, what they are like, how to get into them and what a child (or parents'!) chances are. This is an excellent source of information but a word of warning: don't believe everything you hear. Rumours abound about schools (they are terrible, the children run riot, bullying is rife) and about admission (a certain school is impossible to get into, you have to live on the far side of the High Street to be considered)... and so on. As with all rumours there is usually a grain of truth in each of these... but *not* the whole truth. One parent's negative experience with a school, perhaps experienced many years ago, may be repeated and passed down, eventually being accepted as truth when in fact the school in question has had a new head teacher since that time and has changed beyond all recognition. The same is true about admissions. Don't let one parent's sour grapes about not getting a place for his/her child put you off applying to that school if you believe it is the right one for your child and that you fulfil the criteria.

At the end of the day your child is guaranteed a place at a state school – but you are not guaranteed at which school this place may be offered. All schools will have admissions criteria and an over-subscriptions policy which lays down how they will allocate places should more children apply than they have places available. These are the documents you will need to scrutinise very carefully.

Information about this, and about everything to do with each school, is available in each school's prospectus. These are available upon request (just ring the school and ask to be sent one); you are free to obtain as many as you want, when you want (you don't have to wait until it is time to apply for places and can gather prospectuses from different schools over months or even years, if you so wish). You can also get the same information from your local authority, which will publish booklets each year setting out information about schools (how many places there are, how many people applied in the previous year etc.), together with details about how to apply.

Most of this information will also be available to you through your child's Primary School if you are staying in the same area and, even if you are moving, it is easy to obtain. One of the best sources of information is the Open Evening that most schools put on, usually early in the Autumn term (i.e. during September or early October). This will give you a chance to look round the school, to meet some current pupils and to see examples of pupils' work. Details of how to apply and the criteria for being offered a place are freely available at these events. Some schools require you to apply to your local authority and also to the school directly so it is as well to get all the details clear in your mind. If in doubt, when you have decided which schools to apply to for your child, you can always approach the Admissions Clerk (or whoever that school have put in charge of admissions) who will know the process in detail and who will be able to steer you through.

It is important to be realistic about school criteria. If the school offers places based on academic ability, musical aptitude or sporting skill, for example, it may not be fair to put your child through an application on this basis unless there is a fair chance of him making the grade. Talk to his current classroom teacher (or to his instrument or sports coach if more appropriate) and try to assess whether your aspirations are realistic. It may not be best for your child to have him believe that he has failed in an application to a certain school and is therefore being sent to one that is less good. Such a start is unlikely to be a recipe for success.

Equally it is important to be realistic about yourselves. If, for example, a school requires you to have been regular weekly churchgoers for the last five years – and you know that you only attended services at Easter and Christmas until earlier this year when you discovered the school – it is unlikely to be worth applying. The criteria for schools admissions are required to be fair and transparent and there are all sorts of reasons a school *cannot* give for refusing your child a place. (Full details of these and/or the full School Admissions Code, which came into effect in February 2009, are available from the Department for Children, Schools and Families.) However, this fairness works both ways and parents who are stretching the truth in order to gain a place for their child at a certain school are, increasingly, being found out.

A rough timetable for applying for a place for your child at Secondary School is as follows:

September – Your child begins Year 6 (final year at Primary School). Local Authority application forms become available. Secondary Schools hold Open Evenings where further details of application criteria and process are available. Entrance exams, sports tests and musical auditions may take place if the school uses any of these in their admissions process.

October – Closing date for application forms to be returned to Local Authority and/or schools

November – Fair Banding tests may take place (some schools may have a system where all children take a test on application and then so many places are available in each band. This means that the school admit a 'fair range' of ability levels.)

March (the following year)–The Local Authority and/or school inform parents of their child's place.

Although you will be given an opportunity to put the schools you are applying to in order (i.e. your most desired school first, the next second and so on), the schools should not use where you have placed them to decide whether or not to offer you a place or, in other words, should not only consider 'first choice' applicants. However, if your first choice school does offer you a place, you will not be offered an additional one at your second choice school, so it is important to decide your priorities at the outset.

Should you not be offered a place for your child by the school of your choice, you are free to appeal. Appeals can only be made on the grounds that the school did not follow the published admissions process correctly. Details about how to appeal must be made clear to you at the time when you are declined a place at that school.

All in all the whole process is time-consuming and can be stressful. What is most important is to shield your child from this stress as far as possible. He may already be feeling nervous about the move ahead. If he picks up that you have doubts about how good the school he is moving on to really is it is only going to add to his uncertainty.

Elizabeth says:

"I think the best way to get ideas about what schools are like is to go to open days or activities at that school to get an idea of what the people are like. Are they friendly? Are they helpful? You should decide which school you prefer and then talk about it to your parents. If your parents are really sure they want you to go to a different school you should still be able to discuss it with them. Give them your reasons for your preferred school but try to think these reasons through clearly for yourself. You may just want to go to a school because all your friends are going there but that may not be the right thing for you. In fact it may not even be bad thing to be split up from your old friends because then you get to meet new people and make new friends. You might have found that your old friends became different as soon as they got to Secondary School (like getting into different interests or joining a different group) and you wouldn't have stayed friends anyway. If you are going to be sent to a school you don't want to go to you may be able to

reach a compromise with your parents where you get them to agree that, say, after a year, if you are still unhappy at 'their' school, you could move to the one you want. Talk to your parents about all this – but listen to them too! They probably do have very good reasons for wanting you to go to the school they have chosen."

So what can we do to help?

Before Leaving Primary School:

SATS and assessment

Finding out which school is going to be his next one is only one of the challenges facing the pupil in Year 6. He may or may not have been directly tested as part of the selection process to his new school, but he will nevertheless be facing assessment. He is approaching the end of Key Stage 2 (KS2) and as such his attainment will be recorded to see where he stands in line with national levels.

This assessment may take part through external examination (SATS exams) or – increasingly – through teacher assessment. Either way, this moment of leaving Primary School is one where a snapshot can be taken to see how well he is achieving at various subjects.

Broadly speaking, the target for pupils at the end of KS2 is that they have reached Level 4. This means that if he is assessed as being Level 3 at any subject then his attainment is below the national average; if he is assessed as being Level 5 then he is above. To clarify (or confuse!) things further, each level is divided into three parts (a, b and c, with 'c' being at the lower end of the level and 'a' at the top). So, if you are told that your child has reached Level 4a at maths for example, then he is slightly above the national target and if he is level 4c at writing for example, then he is slightly below.

The main idea of these levels is not to be something that matters so much now but that they are an indication of where he is likely to be when he takes his national exams at the age of 16. The expectation is roughly that a pupil will rise three or four sub-levels every two years. Therefore, if he ends Year 6 with a 4c in writing (i.e. at the lower end of target) this would suggest that he may be a 5c at the end of Year 8, perhaps a 6b at the end of Year 10 and should achieve a Level 7

(or Grade 'C') at GCSE. Of course, children seldo.
this neat pattern. They bound on by several sub-l
year and stay still or even fall back in others. This ma, ue aue
to so many factors – how happy they are, friendship groups,
teaching style, interest, family circumstances, health, puberty...
an almost infinite number of things. All the level at the end of
Primary School really does is give an indication. It can be
helpful in establishing if a child is struggling with a certain
subject and needs extra help or whether he shows aptitude in it
and should be given opportunities to develop this. The
information about his level of attainment in each subject will
be made available to his new teachers at Secondary School and
will be used as a benchmark to assess his progress from that
point onwards.

Like most things the level is designed to be helpful and is
not supposed to be something to worry about or to put extra
pressure on the child. It gives an impartial, factual number on
how well your child is doing in that aspect of that particular
subject but it doesn't say how well he is doing in other aspects
(how confident is he? is he good at getting on with others and

making friends?); nor how successful he is going to be at all the multifarious aspects of his Secondary School.

Some schools have a Transition Officer (a teacher or sometimes a teaching assistant) who visits the Primary School, talks to the child in that context and finds out from his current teachers what his strengths are, his weaknesses, his current attainments and his vulnerabilities. This is, of course, an excellent system but with some schools often admitting 300+ new students each year, often from many different Primary Schools, it is not always possible in every area.

Elizabeth says:

"SATS tests, to be honest, are quite dull. You will probably get loads of practice in them but you should still try your best in them as the results do go with you to Secondary School. However, even if you do badly because you are ill or get really nervous, don't worry. When you get to your new school you will be able to prove that you can do the work after all. Your SATS results are not final results!"

So what can we do to help?

Before Leaving Primary School:

Orientation days

A great way for the pupils to get to know their new school is through orientation days. These are days during the summer term of Year 6 when all the pupils who are going to make up the new Year 7 the following year are invited to the new school for the day. They have a chance to look round, meet some of their new teachers and tutors, use the canteen or lunch hall and generally get used to the routines of the new school. They are usually given various presentations about what to expect when they arrive for real in September. The whole idea is to reassure them and to give them an opportunity to see that the new school isn't really as daunting as it may seem.

This can of course backfire. Sometimes the Year 6s are left to the care of the current Year 7s and it may be that these pupils take a perverse pleasure in telling the new recruits all the horror stories about the school. They tell them about the mountains of homework, the terrifying strictness of the teachers, the terrible punishments meted out should you forget your books EVEN ONCE and the fearful initiation traditions and bullying that goes on to all new pupils. These should *all* be taken with a pinch of salt and most children are astute enough to realise this. It is best to keep an eye on your child during this period though and make sure that you counter any of these (sub)urban myths as they occur. Some children can be scared out of their wits by these sorts of rumours and that is not the idea at all.

Often there will be a number of local schools offering orientation days at different times (sometimes even before the application process begins in an attempt to boost numbers). It is up to you whether you send your child on some or all of them. The visits may allow him to realise that actually all schools are very much the same in the messages they give, the conduct they encourage and the rules they enforce. On the other hand, if you have no intention of your child going to a certain school it may be as well to allow him to stay at his Primary School that day. Certainly you should always be given this option.

Elizabeth says:

"Orientation days are really fun! You get shown round and it is like going to the school but without all the stress. You usually get to meet some of the teachers for the different subjects and you get to meet people from other schools who may be in your year. It is good to go to lots of different schools if you get the chance while you are still choosing schools... just in case you don't get into your first choice school or if your friends end up going to a different school. That way, at least you will know what the other school is like if you do end up going there...or you will understand what your friends are talking about when they start there.

"On the day you will probably be told to wear your normal school uniform (from your Primary School) and to take a small bag with you. In it take a pencil case, a notebook and perhaps your phone. That way if you get lost you can always ring for help – but trust me, you won't get lost! They look after you really well. You might get to try out a couple of lessons, just as a taster but don't worry because they are not testing you. The idea is to give you an experience of the

resources, for example the computers or the machinery in Tech. It is a fun day and you'll probably really enjoy it and be pleased you have had a chance to try out your new school!"

So what can we do to help?

Before Leaving Primary School:

Dealing with anxiety

As your child draws towards the end of his time at Primary School you may find that he becomes increasingly anxious. Moving schools is a major step and it is fair enough for him to be apprehensive. It is important that you take his concerns seriously and that you are prepared to listen to his worries and find ways together to come up with solutions. You may think it all sounds a little childish – but then he is still a child! Eleven is not after all very old and he will be aware that by moving to Secondary School he is joining an environment that is geared primarily for older people. There is a big gap between Year 6, when you are at the top of the school, that school is usually fairly small and you know all the people, where most of the work done by most of the pupils is too easy for you and where you may be familiar with just about every member of the community to Year 7 *and* a new school, where you don't know your way about, you are the youngest, the newest, the least important and where everyone else towers above you, older, more grown up and more confident. Your child is going to have to get used to a new place, new people, new teachers (and different teachers for each subjects rather than one familiar one for all) and new rules. These rules are both overt (those rules that upon breaking, he will be told, will incur fierce penalties) and implied (those unwritten social rules about what you say, what you wear, how you walk that determine if you are 'in or out' in any given group). If *you,* an adult, faced all of this, wouldn't you be nervous too?

One of the sad things that we have to learn as parents is how little we can do to help in this situation. Secondary School is not a place where parents getting involved (or, at least, being seen to get involved) is going to help. Even our advice, even when given quietly in the privacy of our own home, is unlikely to be taken as worth much. Most of the problems of moving school are the problems of growing up and it probably won't be believed that we can know anything about that!

What we can do is provide some consistency, even in the unwelcome things. We need to continue to provide the continuity and security that we have always done. If we have always insisted that our child be in bed by a certain time, we need to continue to do so. We may relent to this time being half and hour later than before – but we still insist. If we have expected our child to help with the dishes or to feed the family pet, we are not going to stop doing so. In this world of change that is threatening to overwhelm him, his boring old parents can stay so comfortingly and reassuringly the same!

Elizabeth says:

"It is natural to be worried – everyone is, so don't think you are the only one out there worrying about your new school. The things most people worry about are teachers (will they be nice?); other pupils (will I make friends?); lessons (will I keep up?); the school size (what if I get lost?); not having the right books (how much trouble will I be in?) and, of course, me (will I make a fool of myself?). Everyone is worrying about all

these things and the answers are that teachers are mostly nice and of course you'll make friends and you won't get lost... and as for books...?!? Come on! It's your first day so no one will expect you to have all the right books just yet!

"Honestly, you won't make a fool of yourself. There are hundreds of new people all making mistakes, so you won't be singled out. Stop worrying and start enjoying this exciting brand new adventure."

So what can we do to help?

Between Schools:

Leaving Primary

For a while, after he has walked out of the door on that last day and before he walks in that new door on the first day of the new-year, your child will not be at school. This happy state of affairs, only dreamed about for so long, may actually come as something of a shock. School may be an inescapable evil for most children, but it makes sense. Not being a member of a school can feel pretty vulnerable and rootless.

As your child, and as his year group, approach this moment they may start to feel this vulnerability closing in. Some children, of course, run out of that door on the last day calling a cheery goodbye and think no further than that tomorrow is the first day of the holidays. For them there is no problem but it is the case that for some children that final day is somewhat traumatic. Usually the school will have built up traditions and techniques to ease this passing and it is best as a parent to go along with them, even if they may seem rather alien to you.

One, which seems to happen in many schools, is the shirt

signing. You may not approve in the abstract but it is fairly usual for the pupils to sign their names and messages of good luck all over each other's shirts on the last day of school. This has become so mainstream that teachers usually join in with the signing and children may even be given allocated times when their class can go round to get signed. The resulting shirt is an important talisman and it is probably best to go along with the tradition and to send your child in on the last day of the year wearing a plain, clean shirt – and one that he has nearly grown out of anyway! There are also likely to be other end of year rituals and events, from sports day to the end of year play, from final assembly and speeches to a school picnic in the playground or the PTA disco in the hall. Each school will be different but if your child has attended that school for some time and has witnessed the previous Years' shenanigans as *they* have gone through all of this, then these events are likely to be seen as pretty important rites of passage and it is probably best to go along with them and take them seriously. These last days are important and they all help to mark the passing from Primary age to secondary. Having said that, this time can become highly emotional and may well leave your child exhausted and upset. It can therefore be a good idea to plan a period of peace and quiet as soon as the holidays have started to allow things to settle down again.

Your child may well leave school promising to stay in touch with a whole cast of people. Many of these may well indeed be moving with him to his new school. Others will drift away as the emotional intensity of the occasion passes, although one or two may (exceptionally!) remain friends for life. Young people have a whole host of ways of staying in touch these days: via the internet; social networking and messaging; through texting and phoning; as well as by *actually* meeting up. It is unlikely, *even* if you have planned to spend the majority of the holidays touring Patagonia, you could seriously affect your child's chances of staying in touch.

Elizabeth says:

"Perhaps you could take in a notebook on your last day and get people to sign it, write messages and phone numbers and addresses. Keep it in a special place, along with your signed shirt, and lots of photographs of the last day. Try to get

photographs of you with your friends, with your class and of course with your teachers. Don't feel like a baby if you cry on your last day. Many people do and it's only natural. After all, you are leaving behind a lot of good memories. Try not to hold on to your old school too much though otherwise you'll just keep comparing your new one to it. Your new school is going to be completely different... and that is a good thing as well as being sad."

So what can we do to help?

Between Schools:

Getting the jobs done

There is no right or wrong way to approach the whole dreaded task of buying all the necessary paraphernalia for the new school but it is perhaps advisable to make sure that you do plan it and make sure you approach it in a way that works for *your* child and *your* family. If your child is feeling anxious, the business of sorting out new clothes, buying new bags and pencil case, updating a mobile phone, buying new sports equipment, having a more grown-up hair style...all these activities can be a way to help face up to *and* face down these anxieties. Making a number of trips out to get these gives you opportunities to focus together on the upcoming move and these may be ideal opportunities for your child to bring up concerns and for the two of you to have time to talk them through together. Spacing the process out over a number of visits might make the whole ordeal less painful for you too (it can all work out to be fiendishly expensive!). On the other hand, there is much to be said too for just getting it over and done with. You don't need the process hanging over you throughout the holiday and there may be additional anxiety caused if, just before the beginning of the new school year, you find that some item on the list is not available. One thing that is certain is that few pupils will want to start the new term looking different and, if everyone else is wearing the regulation jumper with school crest, it is pretty important that you get hold of one for your son or daughter.

Another advantage of shopping early is that you will have plenty of time to sew in nametapes. This quaintly old-fashioned activity is still undertaken all over the country at this time of year, mostly it seems because manufacturers insist on providing their garments with black labels that cannot be written on, however indelible the ink. Perhaps it is true that these evenings spent with needle and thread, nostalgic though they seem, may be one of the more tangible ways we can feel that we are helping our son or daughter in this daunting quest they are facing. Rather like the 'favours' of old, these hand-sewn name labels, representing as they do some hours of time spent in honour of your child, feel like a 'talisman'. Sewing name labels into your child's school clothing is one of those (not!) fondly remembered rites of passage of parenthood. Remember when you didn't know how to fold up a pushchair or install a car booster seat?

The other great thing about getting stuff early is that your child has a chance to get used to it. Practical skills like threading bootlaces, managing mouth guards and tying ties all get easier with a bit of practice. Shoes are more comfortable for a bit of wearing in. Technology, such as a new mobile phone, requires some time for the owner to be confident and familiar with all its functions. Give some holiday time over to familiarising the child with all these things... with familiarity comes confidence!

However, it mustn't be forgotten that this is a holiday. Get all the shopping done, work out how to manage all the new items and get the labelling job out of the way – and then give yourselves some time off. Whatever else it is going to be, the new start is bound to be pretty tiring. Now is the chance to get some rest, go away somewhere to take your minds off the whole thing and to have some fun!

Elizabeth says:

"Try not to fight with your mum or dad while you are out shopping for everything. It may be annoying that she/he is making you spend your holidays out shopping and (worse!) making you think about what is about to happen to you but it is better to get it done… and she/he does understand how you are feeling really. Try to get things like pencil cases that make you feel more confident (perhaps themed around an interest, pop group, television programme etc.) but don't get stuff that is too babyish and will embarrass you when you get there. Also, don't get things that make you look like a total rebel (like with rude slogans etc.) or you will just make your

teachers think you are a trouble-maker and that isn't a very good way to start out!"

So what can we do to help?

Between Schools:

Developing Practical skills

While you are having your time off, and indeed while you are out and about having fun, there is still a huge amount you can be doing – covertly – to help your child with the move ahead. Many of the challenges that will be facing children in their new school environment are to do with increased independence; with making choices and decisions for themselves; with looking after themselves and with keeping safe. Many of these can be practised now with the safety net of your presence still in place.

Some of these skills are fairly mundane yet nevertheless essential. For example, are you sure your child has complete road safety awareness? Can he cross roads safely? manage the cycle to school? (if that is the preferred method of transport); does he know how to catch the bus? Often it is quite 'mechanical' matters like these that are secretly worrying children, so giving them some greater independence over the holiday period may well help to increase confidence. Send him into town on the bus to do some shopping for you. Arrange to meet him on the other side of a strange shopping centre (map provided!). One of the most common reasons for worrying given by children about their new school is getting lost. A bit of practice with various maps and in unfamiliar environments over the next few weeks could really help your child believe that he <u>can</u> do it.

As well as getting himself to the right place in his new school your child is going to have to take greater responsibility for getting there on time. It may sound obvious but can he decipher both analogue and digital time? Is he familiar with the 24-hour clock? If his afternoon lessons begin at 13:55, does he know that this is five-to-two. If a lesson is 45 minutes long, can he work out, quickly and confidently, that he will be finishing the 10:20 lesson at 11:05, leaving himself a ten minute break before the next class at 11:15?

One area that worries many people, not just pupils at a new school, is how to manage lunchtimes. Choosing food, knowing how to manage a cafeteria system, handling money or a debit card… all can be sources of stress. Make sure that you send your child to fetch the lunch during your days out and about. Give him a banknote and instructions that you would like the soup and roll, then take yourself off to the loo! Getting himself in the queue, organising the meals and the tray, collecting cutlery and even choosing a table are all skills that he may need at school, so letting your child have a 'dry run' now is all going to help.

Most of the skills are about being confident in the adult world. Your child, as he hovers between Primary and Secondary School, is hovering also between childhood and adulthood. These are big changes and he is facing huge challenges, as well as a very exciting time. He may need a little encouragement, but chasing him out of the nest and reinforcing that you do believe he will manage perfectly well out there in the adult world will help to give him confidence and establish that, if *you* believe in him, he can begin to believe *in himself.*

Elizabeth says:

"If you are worried about walking to school or catching a bus, you could go once or twice in the holiday while you can still go with your mum or dad and can practise at not getting lost. Arrange to meet your parents at the school and make your own way there so that you know how to do it and how long it takes. If you are going to be dropped off at school, work out where you will be dropped and again work out how long it will take (remember – traffic may be worse in term time). You don't want to be late on your first day but you also don't want to get there stupidly early either or it will just give you more time to get nervous!

Always carry your mobile and make sure that it has some charge and credit. Although at your old school you may not have been allowed to have a mobile, at Secondary it is advisable. Many people leave their phone on vibrate (so that it won't disturb lessons) and leave it switched on all the time. That way you know if you have a message; you can then contact your friends between lessons and arrange where to meet for lunch, whether you are going to clubs and so on. The most important reason for having a phone though is for safety.

If you are travelling home by yourself and you miss your bus, or if you or a friend get hurt or threatened, you can ring for help. Try naming your home number 'I.C.E.' in your contacts list (it stands for In Case of Emergency). That way if you are in trouble or in an accident, or even if you just lose your phone, someone will be able to contact your parents. It is also a good idea to carry a personal alarm – one of those that makes a loud screaming noise if you pull the cord out. This will give you confidence to be more independent and it could even save your life.

So what can we do to help?

Between Schools:

Making and maintaining friendships

Some children moving up to Secondary School are fortunate enough to do so with more or less their complete peer group from Primary School. Others go alone, the only child from that Primary School or even from that area to be going to that particular Secondary School. Either way, it is probably the case that friendships made up until now may well fade anyway.

Although some adults remain close to people they know from pre-puberty, most of us make new friends at this time and it is these friendships, based much more clearly on who we believe ourselves to be, that tend to endure. That said, it is hugely reassuring to have someone to 'move up' with to a new school, even if that person is not someone you are, or would wish to become, particularly close to. This 'moving up together' is not about being soul mates; it is far more about having someone else in the same boat, so that the children can each help each other to find their way around in those all-important early days!

If your child is moving up with a cohort from school this will probably not be a problem. Although most Secondary Schools are 'fed' by a number of Primary Schools so that there will be plenty of new pupils to get to know, pupils are usually put into initial form groups with at least some children they know from their previous school. It might be worth finding out, if you can (often the Primary School, and your son or daughter, will have been told before the end of the year) and perhaps encouraging your child to meet up with someone from this new group over the holidays. They may not have been close friends before but they are going to be thrown together for the first few days at the new school and there is comfort in numbers. Even just arranging to give this other child a lift, or encouraging your son or daughter to arrange to meet up to walk to school together on the first day, can be a great help. Arriving with someone else can give both pupils a bit of courage.

If you are new to the area, or if your child is going to a different school from his previous classmates for whatever reason, this may be more difficult. Sometimes you can manage to find a pupil who is already at the school (but who will be in a different Year...so of limited support) or even someone who is starting the school at the same time. However, given the size of most Secondary Schools, your child and this one may be only two out of three hundred or so, so may not see each other again after they disappear through the doors on the first day. Finding someone who is the right age and the right gender (boys and girls still tend to ignore each other most of the time at this age!), is going to be in the same house or form group and is, in addition, a similar 'type' to your child, is going to be well nigh impossible! You might do better to wait and be ready to nurture the first signs of friendship once your child starts at the school with offers of lifts (and funding!) to the cinema or to the swimming pool. Do not be surprised if your child is very wary about inviting friends home. Home may be regarded as seriously 'uncool' as he or she struggles to forge a 'cool' new identity!

Elizabeth says:

"You will probably find that you make new friends when you get to Secondary School because you will be in new groups and with lots of new people. However, try not to ignore your old friends and keep an eye out for them if any of them are unhappy or finding settling into Secondary School difficult. You may find that if you hang onto your old friends too much though that they make new friends and you get left behind – so try to strike a balance! When you first start at the school it is a good idea to be friendly to everyone but in time there will be some people you like more than others. Try not to make enemies though and try not to leave people out. You will be

meeting different people in different groups and classes and so it is not a good idea to just have one small group of friends or one 'best' friend. Keep an open mind and try to accept some good in everyone (even in boys... or in girls, if you are a boy!)"

So what can we do to help?

Between Schools:

Social 'rules' of Secondary School

Secondary School may involve very different social rules to those your child has abided by up until now. What's more, this is an area in which it is very difficult for you as a parent to be of much help. The start of Secondary School is the start of the teen culture and the end of being just a smaller version of your parents. Moral codes, opinions, political beliefs, looks and even language begin to be things decided by the pupil himself... or more accurately by the peer group with which he allies himself. Before he can decide what sort of person he is going to be as 'himself', he has to first break away from being merely a junior version of his parents and ally himself with people of his own age he feels are 'like him'. This is a complex process and can be painful for both child and parents. All that can be done now though during the holiday between Primary and Secondary is to be alert to, and sensitive to, the quite subtle demands your child may make. Perhaps he insists on grey school shirts rather than white. Perhaps she insists you buy the school jumper several sizes too big or that you buy only long-sleeved blouses that she can roll up. *You* may think that each of these is a) ugly, b) unnecessary or even c) downright foolish but your child won't have hit upon these decisions on a whim. Already his decisions will be based on what he has heard from other children or observed from other pupils at the school or even, if brand new to the area, be based on observations of another school altogether. What matters is that they are the first fledgling attempts to stamp his or her identity on this new institution. They are a way of saying, "This is me!" and, as such – even if to your eyes they are misguided – they matter. Although common sense will delineate your acceptance...("But, mum, everyone at St. So and So's Comprehensive School carries a knife!")... in its more moderate form it may be advisable to go along with it. If it helps build confidence against that dreaded first day, it has got to be good!

Elizabeth says:

"If you know anyone older who already goes to the school ask them to tell you about the things you must avoid (like in our school you MUST NOT do up the buttons of your blazer). Find out what is really best (Tights or socks? Shirt tucked in or out? Sleeves rolled up or down? Trainers or shoes?) and listen to them rather than going on purely what the school prospectus says. This is a great place to start but you will quickly work out your own 'rules' or style. It may be that the person who told you is not someone you particularly want to be like or is someone who is always getting into trouble, so be careful about following anyone else's advice too much".

So what can we do to help?

Going to Secondary School:

The first day

When it comes down to it, you are pretty much powerless to help on the first day. Sure, you have made sure that your child is kitted out with the right clothes (and that they are right in his eyes!), that he arrives at the right time and knows which door to go in through... but beyond that, you just have to let him go. However much of a lump this produces in your throat, this is not the time for tearful farewells, for hugs and kisses, even for secret messages in the lunch box. These things may have worked when you sent him off to Primary School, but they are not what is needed now.

The best parents, on the first day at Secondary School, are the ones who drop their child round the corner from the school and drive off, the ones that send him off to the bus without a backward glance. Tough though it is for us, this adventure is one our children face without us and we are not wanted. Of course, in these days of constant communication it may be perfectly possible for your child to keep in touch via a mobile phone. He may decide to text you (in which case it is okay to answer, if you keep it brief!) but don't initiate contact. However much you are thinking about him and wondering how he is getting on, don't give in to the temptation of sending him a text to ask. The last thing he needs on the first day is to get into trouble for his phone alert going off during class!

At the end of the day your absence, in order for the child to make his own way home or at least so that he can be picked up discretely, is all that is required. Once away from school and safely back in the home your child may well dissolve back into your little girl or boy but it is important that this persona stay hidden from the school environment. Indeed your child may be very childish at home for these first days and weeks. The considerable demands being put upon him or her are likely to lead to great tiredness and the strain of acting in a mature way, and seeking acceptance from new peers, may result in an increase in immature behaviour at home and an exploitation of the unconditional acceptance of loving parents. Perhaps putting up with this with good grace can be one of the ways you help you son and daughter through this transition, however hard that may be on you!

Elizabeth says:

"On the first day try not to do anything that makes you stand out too much. For example, if you fall over and have a massive nosebleed it will tend to draw lots of attention to you which is probably not a good thing (although you can't help falling over!). Try to be 'just one of the crowd', even if this really goes against your nature and you feel a bit like a sheep (...baaa!). You will have plenty of time to assert your individuality later on.

"You will probably start off in your form group and there should be some people there you know or recognise. You might be able to sit with them and chat with them but try to chat to new people too. Make sure you listen and do what you are told. The teachers will be judging you and getting impressions of you and it is best not to be singled out as a troublemaker on your very first day. For example, if you mess about, jiggle about or don't listen (even if this is just because

you are nervous!) they will assume you always behave like that.

"Use your break time and lunchtime to walk around your school and get to know your way around. Try to go with a group of people or play silly games (like one of you going off and then texting the group 'I am in room G42' and seeing if they can find you – a game called 'Lost'). This is a good way of getting to know your way around and getting on with other people. Don't go into places you're not supposed to though like science labs or the sixth form area and don't run if the school rule is to walk in the corridors. If you do get lost for real you could try phoning one of your friends or just ask someone. Everyone is really keen to help the new Year 7s so it won't be a problem.

"Don't worry about the first day. Everyone will look after you really well. It's the second day that is the problem...! Seriously though, you will be given plenty of time to settle in and you won't get into trouble until you've had plenty of opportunity to find your feet."

So what can we do to help?

Going to Secondary School:

Practical support

On a more practical front there are things you can do to help your child make sense of the vast array of information he will be expected to take in during these first days and weeks. He will have been issued with a timetable. This may be little more to him at the moment than a confusing and unrelated series of letters. You can help him bring these into a comprehensible order.

First of all you will need to work out together what his new day looks like. Does he have two or three lessons before break? How long is each lesson? How many lessons does he have then before lunch? How long is lunchtime? How many lessons does he have in the afternoon?

Organising this information onto a form can be tremendously useful. Of course he may have been given a form blank at school although it is just as likely he will have been given a computer printout. Either way, work together on a clear format that is going to make sense to him. Perhaps a large version, which can be pinned up on the board or stuck up on the fridge, may be a practical idea.

Once you have your blank – and thereby have brought the complex and confusing schedule of the school day into a more graspable format – you can add, together, the different lessons, teachers and rooms. Often this will take some decoding if he has been given a printout with mere initials to represent each subject and even more so to work out teachers' names from initials. He is likely to have been issued with a full list of staff, perhaps in his handbook, and now is a great opportunity for deciphering the initials and writing up the full names beside each subject. As for rooms, perhaps colour coding the lesson on the timetable and cross referencing that with the school site map might help your child to get an idea of where things are. Colour coding works well for helping with organisation generally. If Geography is always blue it can be shaded that colour on his timetable, the room can be outlined in blue on the map and homework can be underlined in blue on the day it is set. If your child is encouraged to cover books, these can be colour coded too or the folder that work is kept in can be bought to correspond. All in all there is a fighting chance with all this that your child will have a chance of staying on top of the mountain of organisational challenges that his start at Secondary School will bring.

Another worthwhile task is to go through the school handbook with your child and spend some time discussing the rules. The last thing your child needs is to get into trouble *unintentionally*. Later he may make a conscious choice to break some of these rules ...but that is a different matter! For now it is probably a good idea if both you and he are fully familiar with them. Often pupils get into trouble at school for things their parents have (or haven't) done. If, for example, there is a school rule that homework diaries need to be countersigned by parents each week it is as much your responsibility to do this and it is your child's (although it is fair enough to point out it is his responsibility to remember to bring the relevant book to you!) Similarly, it may be a rule that pupils wear certain footwear; if *you* don't buy this for him he is the one who is going to get told off or put in detention. Checking through the rules together means that you are both then aware of what your obligations and responsibilities are: effectively you are jointly agreeing to do your individual best.

Many schools have Home/School Agreements that you will be encouraged to sign (although these must not be compulsory). Perhaps what you are doing here is recognising that this is a triangle of agreement. The school must keep its side of the bargain and so should your child – but you are making an agreement too, both with the school and with your child, that you will do your best as well.

Often one of the rules is something along the lines that 'pupils will arrive at lessons on time and with the correct equipment to get down to work'. You are helping with the 'on time' part through the timetable and the map; helping with the 'correct equipment' may be down to a system of reminders.

Perhaps your child has a Monday timetable that reads: Maths; Maths; Science; French; History; History; PE; PE. Your child may need help on a Sunday night to ensure that both his maths textbook, workbook and homework are packed in his bag, together with his science books, French books and History folder. He is also going to need PE kit, including perhaps a mouth guard, shin pads etc. If he forgets his calculator or if his games shirt is in the wash and still wet he is going to get into trouble; a bit of help each evening reminding and chiding can make a world of difference… just until he has settled in enough to take full responsibility for himself.

Elizabeth says:

"Pin your timetable up somewhere everyone can see it, like on your fridge, so that your parents can remind you about what books to take and so on (and then you won't feel so nervous when you are getting ready for school). Talk to your parents about school and tell them your teachers names and so on – you can even test them ('What's my English teacher called?'). Try not to 'go into yourself' keeping problems bottled up! Your parents will be keen to help you, at least while you are settling in, so make full use of this. You might even get your favourite dinners if you ask nicely for them! Try not to get all worried at bedtimes… so you can't sleep for going over and over what is going to happen the next day. You have a lot to take in at the moment so it is fair enough to find it all a bit difficult. If you can't sleep sit up and read or listen to music… and, if you are really panicking, go and talk to your parents. Just talking things over sometimes really helps!"

So what can we do to help?

Going to Secondary School:

Homework

One of the biggest areas of dread and of problems tends to be homework. This is for many reasons. For a start your child may be literally tired out at the end of the day and may really struggle to get back down to schoolwork. He may resent this intrusion of school into home life, particularly if he is struggling to settle in and is, at least for the moment, not completely happy in his new environment. He may not have understood what was covered in class or have been unable to accurately record what work should be completed at home and be, therefore, actually unable to complete the work. Teachers may use homework, particularly at the beginning, almost as a way of asserting authority over their charges and may set work almost to test who does, and who does not, complete it. All of these things may lead to considerable strain around that particular subject.

The first thing you can do is to be aware of the issue. If the school has a policy of homework and your child claims not to be being given any, you would do well to be suspicious. Particularly at the beginning of the year, if the school claims to set three half-hour subjects per evening you can be pretty sure that your child should be doing at least some after-school work. Of course it may be that he is completing it in school time and this may be perfectly valid. Many schools offer a lunchtime homework club and your child may well be benefiting from this. However, it is still as well to check the finished result. After all, this is not a case of 'no homework' merely a case of 'homework completed other than at home.'

It may help if you can get into a routine with your child around the end of the school day. This will vary hugely of course according to your own personal circumstances but some sort of settled pattern is likely to help a lot. Perhaps your child will have free time between the end of school and your evening meal, with homework happening after this. Perhaps he will go to a friend, relative or even library at the end of the day before you come home from work and he will do his homework there. Perhaps the rule in your house is going to be that he comes in, has a snack and then gets straight down to work then *before* computer, television or after-school activities are permitted. Every household is different but some formal decision about what is expected is likely to be a good idea. So also is having an agreed place in which to do homework. With laptop computers, as well as pen and paper, it is all too possible for homework to be done on the move, on the bus on the way home or in front of the television. This attitude of getting-it-done-as-quickly-as-possible is only likely to lead to short-term success. Later on in his school life your child will need to do quality work at home that will count towards his qualifications, working independently and in his own time. This is what the daily set homework tasks are leading towards and some support from you in helping your child take homework seriously is likely to pay off in the long term.

You will help your child a great deal if you can become familiar with what work is set and with what work your child is actually doing (which is the reason for the signing of the homework diaries, mentioned earlier). You will also help if you can encourage and even enthuse your child about work set. If you can persuade him that the proper purpose is not so much to merely get it done as to *do it well*, then you are likely to be helping a great deal. There is nothing wrong with having considerable input to help with this process. Of course, doing homework *for* your child is likely to be counterproductive in the long run but doing it *with* your child – at least through showing an interest, reading through the finished piece, perhaps looking things up on the internet or providing relevant books, testing vocabulary or spellings learnt – all are great ways to help. Doing homework alone can be very lonely. Even if all you do is put aside an hour each evening when you too will do some work, check your emails or do your paperwork and bills, the fact that you are working alongside your child may well do much to relieve the loneliness (and thus keep him on task) and so make the issue less likely to be one that ends in conflict.

Finally, your awareness of his homework timetable, as displayed on your board or fridge, can help you remind him when work is due in. Of course, your child at Secondary School is learning to be independent and to take adult responsibility for himself. However, this takes time; if for the first days and weeks (or even months!) you can be there to provide a helping hand and a bit of a nudge you will probably help this process along nicely.

Elizabeth says:

"Nobody likes homework! We all have to do it so it is just as well to get on with it and get it over with. For the first few days at your new school you shouldn't have much homework but it will start to be set soon enough. Don't avoid homework by not doing it or you just fall further and further behind and end up getting into trouble.

"Not all homework is horrible. Sometimes it can be a project like making a model or recording a radio play with your friends. Some of these things can be done in school time, at break or lunch or after school and there is usually an actual homework club in school where there are teachers there to help you if you get stuck.

"If you don't understand a homework, ring a friend from that lesson and try to find out what it is all about or you could ask your parents or ask a teacher the next day. It isn't a good idea to leave it until it is due in or they will just think you are trying to get out of doing it. As long as you show that you are trying to do it, you should not get into trouble."

So what can we do to help?

Going to Secondary School:

Dealing with 'fall-out'

It is worth being aware in advance that at some point during these first Secondary School days your child is quite likely to fall apart. Initially she may be doing well, may come home positive about the new classes and teachers and even perhaps be excited and enthusiastic about her homework. This may continue throughout the first week or even two and you may heave a sigh of relief and reckon that the whole move has gone remarkably smoothly. What was all the worry about?

...and then the storm breaks! Your child falls out with new 'friends'. She forgets to do homework and panics on the day it is due in, feigning illness and screaming in fury when you refuse to allow her to stay at home that day. She becomes stroppy, unhelpful or tearful, fights with her younger brother, refuses to wash her hair, tears his much-loved poster off her bedroom wall – and you find yourself quite suddenly in a war zone.

This sort of meltdown is not unusual nor is it, really, terribly unexpected. We can all of us cope with considerable strain for short periods of time. However it may have seemed, the changes of the move to Secondary School are a considerable strain and your child may well have been managing on a kind of short-term adrenaline. What's more, she is not alone. All of her peers, the ones she knows well and the new pupils she has never met before now, are similarly coping by the skin of their teeth and this may well lead to a pretty volatile school environment. When everyone is feeling fragile, it is all too easy to fall apart! Even (and this is a seldom admitted fact!) the teachers will, to a certain extent, have been living on borrowed time. These first days and weeks are not a true reflection of what being at a school is like. Any class can behave itself for the first few sessions as it sizes up the teacher and any group of children or adolescents can get along while they are working each other out. Then comes the beginning of the need to assert themselves. Those who want to lead or dominate will begin to do so, both over their peers and (at least in attempt!) over their teachers. Groups of students who clung together for company in early days of nervousness begin to break apart, often quite ruthlessly, as one group sheds members they decide not to tolerate. Teachers who begin to feel their early easy control of a class slip away may well become considerably tougher, issuing punishments or detentions to all who stray off the path, even those who do not mean to. Your child may become genuinely frightened of staff who shout or who become excessively angry. She may suffer from loneliness and rejection if the group she first joined move on without her. She may feel a failure socially or academically as pupils make choices about whom they will sit with, whom they will hang out with at break, whom they will join for lunch. She may start to lose the easy understanding of a subject and to realise she is slipping behind or that she is not going to be able to cope with a certain group or setting. Those easy early days, when everyone was new and you weren't expected to know anything, may begin to seem like a far-off dream.

Very often it is the parents who bear the brunt of this. A pupil may get through the school day with the problems being (just) manageable but when she gets home, they may overwhelm her. Shouting, raging and crying at your parents can be a huge relief. Acting unreasonably, even rudely, painting the darkest picture of failure and rejection *and still being loved* can be a wonderful safety valve. Sometimes a child will *just need* to do this, to be utterly horrible and despairing, in order to get the energy together to face the following day. Parents have to deal with fall-out: it goes with the territory.

It is worth bearing in mind that much of this will pass. While it is true that there is often a turbulent time at this stage of the year, just as there is a 'honeymoon' period at the very start, it is also true that things do, very quickly, start to settle down again. Your child is likely to be very tired and therefore less able to cope than usual. Small knocks that she would usually take in her stride may well grow into big ones in her mind and she may feel that everything is going wrong when in fact this is far from the truth. Perhaps the most welcome and needed break in the school calendar is that first half-term! If she, and you, can stagger through to it, the chance to sleep and recuperate could well put a great many of the problems that threaten to overwhelm back into perspective.

Elizabeth says:

"When you feel grumpy and like you can't cope try not to take it out on your family or your friends. Try to do something like taking a long bath or watching a film or playing your favourite computer game for a while to take your mind off it. Try to work out what it is that's bothering you and try to find a way around it. If it is nothing definite, you are probably just tired. Perhaps you could miss going to a club or a voluntary after-school activity – just for that week – to give yourself a chance to have a rest and catch up with yourself."

So what can we do to help?

Going to Secondary School:

Settling in

One of the questions you will probably want to ask yourself is how soon you can relax and reckon that the move to Secondary is over. Is half-term a reasonable target? If you can all stagger this far, can the move be said to have been completed? The issue is that, although the vast majority of pupils will settle down after the move as happy and confident members of their new school, for a few the problems to do with *moving* to Secondary become problems to do with *being* at Secondary. As the next section of this book describes, even after the initial move has passed and the child has settled down that does not mean the end to all problems or issues for any pupil. There will still, of course, be much that parents need to do.

What this half-term break does do is to signal the end of the transition problems. It signals a point after which most pupils will go back to the school as fully integrated members of that school. It is the first of the holiday periods, a time to take stock and, after a chance to rest and recover a bit, to look back on how far you have come. Most Year 7s wouldn't recognise themselves from the frightened children they were just a few short weeks before! Sometimes the half-term break gives a chance to go back and visit the Primary School, particularly if holiday dates are different. The response to this is almost always, "Isn't it SMALL?!!?" It is only when the direct comparison is made with how things *were* that the young person realises just how much they have moved on and grown up.

This is a great point for the Primary School to make use of these reflections. If Year 7s could be encouraged to feedback to Year 6s just what the experience of moving really is like, especially now while it is all so fresh in the mind and while the individual is feeling a real sense of success, this information would be of great value to the next Year group when they too approach this time. It is a shame that this opportunity is seldom practical to organise in a formal way.

For a few pupils, of course, the problems that persist become less to do with not knowing the routines or where to go, not knowing the people or misjudging their requests or expectations, and more to do with knowing each of these and yet still not being happy with them. However careful, prepared and diligent you were in choosing the school for your child, no one can really know what a school is like until they experience it from the inside and no two pupils' experiences will be precisely the same. As the detail of what life at Secondary School is really like becomes clear, your child may *not* be able to adjust. For parents, this can be extremely difficult. What if you have diligently guided your child across to this 'brave new world' only to find that it actually proves – in practice – not to be where he, or, for that matter, you, yourself, now wish him to be?

Elizabeth says:

"You know you are starting to settle in when you don't wake up in the morning and have a first thought that is, 'Oh no – I've got school!' You may never wake up and think, 'Oh great!', but you should start to have something each day to look forward to, a lesson you like or just seeing your friends. If you never have a day that has something good in it, or if there are things each day that you are actively dreading, then it may be necessary to tell your parents that you are really not happy. There is probably something that can be done to make things better but not if you don't let on to someone in authority that there is a problem."

So what can we do to help?

Being at Secondary School:

Dealing with continued anxiety and unhappiness

If your child doesn't settle in and begin to enjoy school within the first few weeks you are going to have to give added support. For the vast majority of children the idea of the move to Secondary School is far more daunting than the actual experience but, for a few of them, being at Secondary School is not easy and they do not find that they feel at home. This may be because of quite specific problems, for example: bullying, taunting or exclusion from the social group; because of fear or dislike of a certain teacher; because of perceived inability in a certain subject *or* it may be a more general, amorphous feeling that they just don't fit in.

Your problem is going to be finding a way to get to the bottom of what the problem really is. It may well not be what your child says it is. For example, saying a certain teacher 'hates me' may be in reality an issue of confidence in that subject or could be because another pupil in that class is being unpleasant. Saying he 'hates PE' may be an issue around taunting in the changing room as much as about the subject itself. It may well be that your child feels that whatever is troubling him is his own fault or is shameful in some way and you are going to have to be both sensitive and tenacious if you are to find a way to help.

What is almost certain is that your child will believe that you cannot help. Because Secondary School is somewhere you go without your parents, because it is somewhere where you are supposed to practise independence and where you are supposed to begin to be able to sort difficulties out for yourself, there seems to be little room for parent intervention. Although this is true, it is important that your child can still believe that ultimately you can keep him safe. He must be able to trust that you will believe him, and that you will take his concerns seriously. He will also need to know that you won't do anything to intervene without discussing it with him first. Nothing is more worrying than the fear that your parents will step in, embarrass you and quite simply make the whole situation worse than ever.

Reassure your child that you are worth confiding in, that you will understand his point of view, that you will only act after discussion with him and that, ultimately, you have his best interests at heart and have the power to protect him as necessary. It depends on your own family circumstances but there may be a case for reassuring your child that, if he continues to be actively unhappy or afraid, and if the situation cannot be resolved, then he need not stay at that school. Of course, promises like this are hollow if you cannot deliver on them if the need arises so you may need to think clearly about what circumstances would be required for you to withdraw your child. It will probably never come to it and it is almost certainly the case that problems *can* be sorted out and issues resolved but perhaps you, and your child, *need* to have the reassurance of a worst case scenario that allows your child an 'out'.

Elizabeth says:

"There is always a reason for being unhappy. You don't just feel unhappy – there is always going to be something that is causing it. You need to work out in your own mind what the problem is and then tell someone you trust – your parents or

your form teacher. You might not think that there is anything that can be done to help but there probably is if you just trust them."

So what can we do to help?

Being at Secondary School:

Bullying

One of the biggest fears about Secondary School is that of bullying and it should always be taken seriously as an issue. Although there is less of it in reality than urban myth would have your child believe, bullying does exist in some form, at some time at every school and it can have devastating consequences on its victims. If you fear that your child is being bullied, *always* take it seriously and *always* act. If your child is being victimised it is already out of control and it is unlikely that he or she will be able to put the situation right without help. You cannot just trust to the hope that bullying will stop by itself: it *needs* to be stopped.

All schools will have an anti-bullying policy and that is a good place to start. Read it carefully and make sure that you know what the school is ready to do to help. Go through it with your child, and make clear notes about what is happening: the where, the when and the how. Although it is difficult, it is likely to be a help if both you and your child can step back from the situation and view it dispassionately. Concentrate less on why what is said or is done is hurtful and more on why it is wrong. For example kicking or punching someone is an offence termed *Assault.* Comments that are racist, sexist or discriminate against someone for their beliefs, sexual orientation or because of a difference or disability are recognised as wrong in law. You don't have to prove that something is hurtful or damaging: that proof is already self-evident.

You and your child have rights to go about your business free from threat or intimidation. These rights are empowering and help victims of intimidation – of bullying – to realise that this is not their fault. Knowledge of your rights will also help counter the fear that nothing can be done to stop intimidation. Stopping bullying is hard and can take considerable time and effort but it can be done and it is your child's right that it *should* be done. Never let the authorities at the school tell you that they have done all they can. They know that they have a statutory obligation to do everything possible until the bullying is stopped.

Of course, you may not know your child is being bullied as children who are victims may feel ashamed and guilty and will have been told that no one will believe them and that there is nothing that can be done. They may have been threatened that 'grassing-up' will bring further retribution. Your child may be too frightened or too embarrassed to talk to you about the issue. You can be vigilant to bullying by being aware of your child's weekly (or fortnightly) timetable. It may be that a certain day triggers the tantrums the night before, the arguing and misbehaving that evening or the complaining of sickness or ill health as an attempt to be allowed a day at home. Although it can be difficult to decode, see if there is a correlation between this type of behaviour and certain factors. It may be that the trouble is happening in a certain lesson with a certain group of people.

It may be that it happens on Tuesdays and Thursdays when your child has PE. It may happen on days when she catches the bus or when her form are on first lunch sitting. It may take considerable detective work but you may be able to deduce something of what the problem is in this way. On the other hand, of course, the problems could be happening randomly or even daily so that no pattern emerges. In this case, all you will have to go on is your child's general misery. Try to get her to confide in you or if not in you then in another relative or friend. Although she won't believe it, there are things that can be done. Bullying *can* and *must* be halted. Your child must not be afraid to go to school.

Elizabeth says:

"In most schools bullying is NOT tolerated and in fact there is not nearly so much of it as some people fear. However, it does still happen in some cases and you need to know what to do if you, or if one of your friends, gets into this situation. There are many different types of bullying, from a few snide words to actual punching and kicking. Usually bullying involves peer pressure (e.g. making you do something you don't want to do) and laughing at people or not including them. If you are left out once or twice, don't count this as bullying as it could just be that your friends are busy with something else or are just

having a bad day. Bullying that goes on, or that is frightening or upsetting you, is serious though and you shouldn't be afraid to tell a teacher or your parents, even if the people bullying you tell you not to. Telling on bullying is not snitching – it is sorting things out for yourself and being responsible, which is what Secondary School is all about.

When you tell a grown-up, most times the grown-up will be able to sort it out quietly and no one will even know that you have been to them. Often the bully is doing what he or she is doing for a reason, like unhappiness at home or a feeling of not doing well at school Because of this it is not really a good idea to come back at them, when they are unpleasant, with a clever retort or comment. If you put them down they are likely to come back at you harder than ever. One response is to, say, agree but without putting yourself down and then to say something nice to them. For example, if a bully laughs at you for your artwork done in class it might work to smile, agree that art isn't your best subject (implying that other things are) and tell her that her painting is really good. This is often the last thing she expects or is used to. Another reaction that you are often told is just to ignore the person, which is fine up to a point, but don't think it means you have to put up with bullying. You should always tell a grown-up if you feel bullied and that grown-up should always do something about it.

On no account get into a situation where you become a bully yourself. Sometimes it can be tempting to get a laugh from your friends by saying something unkind or 'clever' about someone else but it is not worth it. Bullies ALWAYS lose in the end."

So what can we do to help?

Being at Secondary School:

Talking to the school

Talking to your child and finding out what is wrong is going to be your first step, regardless of whether the problem turns out to be bullying or something else. There may be strategies you can suggest to deal with whatever is bothering your child but it is also quite likely that you will need to talk to the school to get whatever issues emerge sorted out. How you do this needs to be agreed with your child.

Most schools offer some sort of tutor group system, where your child's pastoral care is managed by someone who may be completely apart from those who teach him. Sometimes these tutor groups are arranged in Year groups although in other schools they are arranged in what is known as 'Vertical Tutoring', where a tutor group has members from each of the school's Year groups. The advantage of this is that the tutor can give more individual attention to the different needs of the various age groups (for example, giving advice on subject options in Year 9, helping with exam timetables in year 11 and working on university applications etc. in Year 13). It can also work well that the older students look after the younger ones in their tutor group – but it can also be the case that it leads to individuals being isolated, away from peers and peer support.

If your child has developed a good relationship with his or her tutor, this could be a good place to start. Ask for an appointment and go in to discuss your concerns. You could take your child with you for this meeting or you could go alone but it is important that your child is aware of the meeting and about what will be discussed. Try to keep your concerns specific and concentrate on what your child's problems are, rather than worrying about what the school can do to help. That is their problem! You may not be able to see any way forward with a particular problem or issue but your child's tutor should be able to and, if he or she can't, will have to consult further to find a solution. Always agree what the next course of action is going to be and agree a timetable for when the problem will be addressed. It is a good idea to write a short note after the meeting to thank the tutor for his or her time and to record what you have agreed. Keep a copy of this and then if the problem is not resolved you will be in a stronger position to take the matter further.

The last thing you want to be with your child's new school is confrontational. It is worth bearing in mind that schools are busy places and, during the highly concentrated school day, time is a scarce commodity. With this in mind, it is unrealistic to expect your child's tutor to talk to you without an appointment or to take telephone calls when he or she may well be teaching at that time. However, it is also worth accepting that individual matters *do* get forgotten or shelved in busy lives and it may be necessary for you to be calm and polite yet tenacious if your concerns are going to be properly addressed. Remember that if your child *is* unhappy you have a right to get whatever is making him unhappy sorted out, so *don't* be put off.

Finally, your child's tutor is not going to be the only person you can turn to. Schools may have any number of people from Pupil Support Officers and Heads of House, through Counsellors and the School Nurse, to Parent Advisers or Heads of Year. Ultimately, there are the Head Teacher, the Governors and the Education Authority. If you are unwilling (justifiably!) to give up, you must believe that any problem your child is experiencing can be resolved by someone. You just have to keep trying!

Elizabeth says:

"If there is something at school that you feel you can't sort out for yourself, try getting your parents to write you a letter on the subject to take with you when you go to see the teacher. Many schools have a Pupil Support Manager whose job it is to sort out pupils' worries and concerns, but it can be difficult just to go and see this person yourself. A letter from your parents helps show that your parents are behind you and that

they are taking the problem seriously but they are still supporting you to sort it out for yourself. The next step, if that doesn't work, is for your parents to make an appointment to go in to see a senior member of staff. If you have already been to see the Pupil Support Manager, and have had a letter from your parents too, this will help to show that the matter is serious and that you have tried to sort it out for yourself first. "Try not to rely on your parents too much, especially for the little stuff, because you are going to have to learn to manage problems for yourself. Look on your parents as your back-up or a last resort who will be there if you really can't manage. However, don't try to dissuade your parents from going into school if you do need them to – just because you feel embarrassed! They are not going to march in and start shouting in assembly! Agree with them how and when they will go in to school and what they will say. You should go with them if at all possible."

So what can we do to help?

Being at Secondary School:

The 'wrong crowd'

Sometimes, of course, it is not your child who is unhappy at all: it is you! It may be that your child has settled in beautifully to the new school but has become unrecognisable to you. She may have made friends with people who are constantly in trouble or he may have stopped doing any work at all and his levels of achievement may be plummeting. What do you do now?

Although this is a problem for you, rather than for the school, it is still something you can tackle together. If you feel his work has suffered, agree with his teachers that a certain level has to be achieved or that they have your full support to keep him in detention. Agree that details of assignments will be emailed across to you so that you can make sure that they are completed. If your child has made friends with pupils who are constantly in trouble, make sure that she know that you will not accept rude or defiant behaviour. Again, work with the teachers, making it clear that they have your full support.

Agree sanctions that can be implemented at home – withdrawal of spending money, refusal to pay for trips, 'grounding' – and communicate with teachers to make sure that behaviour is acceptable to you both. If you and the school put up a united front, and have agreed expectations of behaviour and work, there is every chance you will succeed.

If your child is aware that you and the school are working together to enable her to achieve her full potential and that both you and the school believe in her and believe that all this effort is worthwhile, it is quite likely that, in spite of the odd grumble, she will accept it. She might even (secretly) be quite pleased!

Elizabeth says:

"You need to decide for yourself what the 'wrong crowd' really is. It may be that your parents don't approve of a group of your friends but you trust and value them and still want to be with them. On the other hand, your parents may not like a crowd for quite good reasons – like because they take drugs or skip school or because they are in trouble with the police etc. In this case your parents have a good point so it is important

not just to be stubborn and refuse to listen to them as a matter of principle.

If your parents think your friends are the 'wrong crowd' but they are people you want to remain friendly with, you could try to show your parents that you are able to be trusted to make your own decisions. Act responsibly around the house, don't throw temper tantrums and become rude and unreasonable and make sure you still do your school work... and your parents will probably be fine about it. They will only think your friends are the 'wrong crowd' if your behaviour changes and gives them cause to start worrying."

So what can we do to help?

Being at Secondary School:

Defiance and trouble

Having said all of this, some defiance and trouble are probably to be expected. Your child has gone to Secondary School and is starting to grow up. Part of this is pulling away from parents and family and finding ways to be more independent. Disagreeing with your parents is really quite a healthy step on the road to adulthood.

It is important that you are able to distinguish between this normal healthy defiance and the anger that comes from unhappiness. It is important to differentiate between normal teenage moodiness and mood swings that originate from depression, alcohol or drugs. It is essential that, while your young teenage child pulls away from you, you remain rock-like and reliable, that you impose rules that keep your child safe even though they are moaned about and that you are there, to be turned to and to offer support and love, whatever your child does. Bringing up children is a challenging experience and no one said that having a child at Secondary School was going to be easy. It is okay to accept that finding the experience exhausting, unrelenting, confusing and frustrating (as well as ultimately rewarding and wonderful) is perfectly usual!

Elizabeth says:

"'No' is a word that you may find your parents saying quite a lot over these years but that is to be expected. They are just trying to protect you. If you say you want to go to a party for example they will probably say 'No' until you can convince

them. Convincing them is done by being responsible, always being home and/or phoning home when you say you will and generally reassuring them that they needn't worry about you. They may seem to be horrible killjoys, but actually they love you. Try to negotiate and you should be able to come up with a solution that is acceptable to you both."

So what can we do to help?

Being at Secondary School:

Your ongoing support

...and, of course, it doesn't end there! Even after your child has settled fully into Secondary School life, and is coping with the emotional and physical upheavals of growing up, there are plenty of minefields ahead. As regards schooling, these tend to come at the end of Key Stages. At the end of Key Stage 3 (Year 9) your child is likely to face subject options. This is when he makes the decisions that will affect the rest of his life (...no pressure there, then!) and decides which subjects to study to exam level.

He may have to make some fairly fundamental decisions about himself:

* ❖ Is he an academic person who is likely to go on to higher level education?

* ❖ What subject(s) may he study there and what subjects now does he need to follow in order to do so?

* ❖ Is he someone with a particular interest or skill?

* ❖ Is he planning to concentrate on a particular sport or to study music?

* ❖ Does he need to work on computer skills, to improve language skills, to work in a particular vocational direction?

The list of questions is almost inexhaustible...

In fact, although he will need your support during this decision-making process, many of the decisions may be made for him. The school may more or less be channelling him in a certain direction – which is fine if that is really where he wants to go. By now the school should have a fairly realistic understanding of his potential in various areas but that does not always mean that they know best. Be aware that if your child is particularly good at a subject, staff may well be very keen for him to continue to study that subject with them. That is usually an excellent decision but just occasionally it might mean pulling a child in a direction in which he really doesn't want to go. Parental expectation can work in this way too. Perhaps you have always dreamed of your child going to university and have been saving towards this great day for years. Are you willing to *really* listen when he tries to explain that what he really wants to do is to get some practical experience working at what he *really* wants to be: a chef, a car mechanic, a sword-swallower in the circus...?

Another time when parents are going to be needed to give support is during exams. We live in a culture where constant examining has become the norm and it may seem to us that yet another GCSE test in Geography is not that much to get excited about. However, considerable strain can be put on young people to prove themselves through the exam results they obtain. Expectations may be ridiculously high and it is important that students are given plenty of support during this time.

They may need help organising revision time and juggling different deadlines for completed assignments. They may need help going over revision notes or organising their material in a way that makes it easier to memorise. They may need help just getting regular meals and plenty of sleep. Sixteen (or even eighteen) is not really very old. Even when our children come to the end of their time at Secondary School there is likely to still be a huge amount that we can do to help them. ...and then...*seemingly in the blink of an eye...* it is time to start thinking about supporting them on their move onto work or travel or college but that is another book!

This one has just about come to an end. I hope it has helped both you as a parent and your child. There are huge challenges and obstacles to overcome when your child moves to Secondary School but on the whole there is one big secret that no one ever seems to tell you: that it is fun! Growing up is great! Watching your child blossom into a young man or woman and always being there for him or her (sometimes discreetly, sometimes more proactively!) is also great... in spite of all the worries and the pitfalls.

Enjoy it!!!

A final word from Elizabeth:

"Before I went to Secondary School I was worried about getting lost and about not being with my friends. I was worried as well that if I didn't keep up in the lessons then I might get moved down a group. I remember I was worried about detentions too, because everyone kept going on about them and we didn't have detentions at Primary School.

"I think, looking back, that the Orientation Day helped me most because I was worrying about what it was all going to be like but on the Orientation Day I got to meet people in my Year. I got to meet a lot of my teachers and I was even given some basic equipment too like a planner and a map. I got to learn some basic facts about the school and everyone was really friendly and helpful.

"I had a visit to my Primary School from the Head of Year 7 but it was a bit daunting meeting him on my own! He wanted me to ask questions but I didn't want to sound insulting so I couldn't ask things I really wanted to know – like 'Is it a nice school?'! He did tell me basic things like the shape of the timetable, when break and lunch are and things like that. He talked to my old teacher, too, so I knew that he would have found out about me, like what my learning attitude was and things like that.

"It helped too that people came in from other Secondary Schools to talk to us as you can take some basic details from any school, because most of the rules and so on are much the same. People asked questions in those sessions and it was easier to ask when there were lots of people there and it wasn't just me on my own.

"I think it would have helped if I could have met the pupils from nearby Primary Schools who were going to the same Secondary School so I could have got to know them a bit and wasn't just surrounded by a crowd of unknown faces; perhaps even if they could have emailed us pictures or even names of other pupils or set up a website where we could have 'met up' in a chatroom. It would have been brilliant too if some of the Year 7s who were already there (who were going to be year 8s by the time we got there) could have come to talk to us and tell us a bit about what to expect. Maybe sixth formers would have been good too like the ones who were going to be our form *helpers. They could have come in and reassured us that they would be there to help us when we started for real.*

"My advice for during the holidays, between schools, would be that if you've got a timetable you should try to learn the week of lessons so you don't feel so unprepared. Go and buy all your uniform and equipment and have it in your room so you can look at it and get used to it. That way, gradually, it won't feel so alien to you.

"On the first day find some people you recognise (even if just from the Orientation Day) and that will make you feel less alone. Don't just stick with one person though but try to widen the group you go around with. This will make it less likely you will fall out with friends and also, should a particular friend be put in a different group, less likely you will be left on your own. It is better to be friendly with lots of people and to be ready to make new friends.

"The main difference between Primary and Secondary School is the size of the school, but actually that's really easy to get used to because really you still have the same number of people who matter to you as you did before. You have your circle of friends and your teachers and the fact that all the other people

are there doesn't really matter that much. It is quite hard to find your way around but your teachers do understand and lots of people are there to help you. Schools are often in blocks so once you get the hang of something being 'in the Humanities block', for example, the way round becomes a lot easier to work out.

"Work is quite hard but it is set at a standard and at a progress rate that suits you so it is possible to keep up (I expect I learnt that from talking to our previous teachers). Homework IS as bad as they say (ugh!!!) although teachers don't give you half as much as some people claim they do before you start. I haven't had a detention (so far so good!!!) and neither have most people I know. People go on about them before you start but actually it's quite rare to get detentions and teachers have other, less serious sanctions they use first.

"What I wish I had known is that actually it is all quite good fun. You settle in really quickly and soon get into the routine of the school. Very soon you feel just as much at home as you did at your old school and you also feel more confident, more trusted and more independent. I hope YOUR move up to

Secondary School goes well. Good luck with it all and I hope you REALLY, REALLY, REALLY enjoy your new school!"

INDEX

INDEX

Emerald Publishing

www.emeraldpublishing.co.uk

106 Ladysmith Road
Brighton BN2 4EG

Other titles in the Emerald Series:

Health
The Ultimate Nutrition Guide for Cancer Sufferers - *Zoe Hellman*
The Ultimate Nutrition Guide for Joint and Arthritic Conditions -
Zoe Hellman
Understanding Depression - *Nicolette Heaton-Harris*
A Guide to Alternative Health and Remedies - *Jenny Halbert*
Mental Health & the Community Part 1 - *Marianne Richards*
Mental Health & the Community Part 2 - *Marianne Richards*
Asthma begins at home - *Rosie Gordon*
Finding Asperger Syndrome in the Family - *Clare Lawrence*
Children's Health Combating Obesity - *Nicolette Heaton-Harris*

New Perspectives
Writing True Crime - Stephan Wade
Being a Professional Writer - Stephen Wade & Kate Walker
The Music Industry - Teri Saccone
Writing the Perfect C.V. - Caroline Temple
Damage Rendered - Johnny Richards
What Children Learn in the Classroom - Kate Stewart

Busines titles
A Busy Managers Guide to Managing Staff - Lynda MacDonald
Keeping Books and Accounts - Colin Richards
Business Start-up and Future Planning - Gordon Clark
Health and Safety - Law and Practice - Samantha Walker

For details of the above titles published by Emerald go to:

www.emeraldpublishing.co.uk

CHILDREN'S HEALTH
COMBATING CHILD OBESITY

A Comprehensive Guide to Children's Health and Fitness Children's Health-Combating Obesity, is an extremely comprehensive guide to the problems affecting children and their health from the early years through to the teens.

The book specifically approaches the problems of obesity, dealing with causes and effects of obesity, both medical and psychological, and providing a series of healthy diets and activities which will ensure that a child grows up healthy and fit and avoids the dangers inherent in the early years.

The book covers the following areas in detail:

Facts about child obesity
Effects of obesity
Medical causes of obesity
Motivation and Self-Esteme
Healthy and enjoyable food programs
Activities to combat obesity
Involving the child in choice

The Author. Nicolette Heaton Harris is an author and expert in the areas of child health and child psychology. She has published three books in this area, on teenage pregnancy and mental health. This book follows two years of research into child health and the causes of obesity.

Pub: May 2007   ISBN 1847161239   £9.99

FINDING ASPERGER SYNDROME IN THE FAMILY
A Book of Answers by Clare Lawrence

This recent book in the Emerald Series, is a comprehensive and clear guide to Asperger Syndrome and the effects on children and family.
Not everyone facing this issue for the first time is ready for complicated hard to digest material. This book is invaluable in that it takes the form of providing key answers to questions which are most often raised and is aimed at the absolute beginner in this field. It will prove invaluable to all those who wish to understand more about this complex area, whether parent or professional.

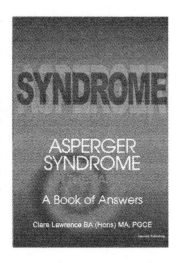

The following areas are covered in detail:
- o Sensory issues
- o Interventions
- o Behavioural problems
- o Diet
- o Drugs
- o Educational issues
- o Explanation of symptoms and description of conditions

The author. Clare Lawrence BA (HONS) MA PGCE has a postgraduate certificate in the area of Aspergers Syndrome. Her own son was diagnosed with AS four years ago and she has become heavily involved in the educational aspects of AS. She was involved as a parent at the inception of the DASLne Autism Database in the north-east and she appears on the Great Ormond street educational DVD about more effective early diagnosis of AS.

Emerald Publishing   ISBN 184716 008 5   £8.99

ASTHMA BEGINS AT HOME
Help Yourself to a Healthier Future by Rosie Gordon

Asthma Begins at Home is an approachable guide for asthmatics and their families. It is a positive first step towards understanding and taking control of allergic disease. We are hearing more and more about the increases in asthma, with questions about asthma littering the daily press. In the UK alone, over 5 million people are living and dying with this debilitating disease today. In the UK, serious or life threatening asthma results in 74,000 emergency hospital admissions each year. Currently, 1,500 people die from asthma each year, over a third of which are people over the age of 65. Asthma attacks now cost the UK an estimated £1.2 billion in lost productivity, £850 in NHS treatment and a further £1.6 million on social security costs. (2001 Asthma Audit by the National Asthma Campaign). Nell Nockles was very nearly another victim of asthma, until she discovered the effects of removing allergens from her environment. She has since devoted her life to research and campaigning for the public to share this vital information.

The Author. Rosie Gordon is a writer and editor and has been a part of the Nockles family campaign for seven years. She has been involved in channelling their research into the unique, educational website www.housedustmite.org , which gets over 400 visitors a day. Asthma begins at home: Clearly explains allergic asthma without drowning you in science Challenges the efficacy of current asthma treatment Looks at your environment as the cause of symptoms Explains that you are in control of your health gives clear, simple guidelines for improving symptoms Includes feedback from a study group which tried these methods. Revised Edition May 2007

Emerald Publishing   ISBN 1847 160 26 3   £9.99

A PARENTS GUIDE TO PRIMARY EDUCATION

In The Classroom - A Parent's Guide to Primary Education is a user friendly, at a glance, guide for parents to what their children are taught at primary school.

It gives a brief description of the more modern teaching methods so that parents can gain a familiarity with, and an understanding of, the processes that their child will go through in the primary school setting. The book covers the development of numeracy, literacy and the wider curriculum from when children enter school in Reception at age 4, through Key Stages One and Two until the move to secondary school at age 11. It gives parents an insight to what - and how - their children are learning, and suggests a wealth of ways to support that learning at home.

The book covers the following areas:
- o Numeracy
- o Literacy
- o The wider curriculum
- o Key stages of development
- o Helping at Home
- o Moving to Secondary school

The author. Kate Stewart - Kate is a teacher, a school governor and a writer on education. Most importantly she is a parent of two children at primary school and is able therefore to give a parent's perspective on understanding and supporting learning during these important years.

Kate Stewart   ISBN 184716 078 6   £8.99

FAMILY LAW
A Comprehensive Guide to Family Law Including the Law of Divorce

This first book in the Emerald Home Lawyer Series, Family Law, is clear and concise and is intended for the professional, the student or the layperson.

It is ideal for anyone who wishes to develop their understanding of this complex area.

The book is comprehensive and covers the following areas in detail:

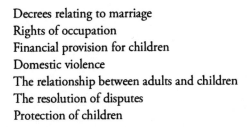

Decrees relating to marriage
Rights of occupation
Financial provision for children
Domestic violence
The relationship between adults and children
The resolution of disputes
Protection of children

Revised Edition May 2007

Emily Broadhurst   ISBN 1847 16 025 5   £9.99